Genre Folktale

MW00489602

Essential Question
What choices are good for us?

Finn MacCool and the Salmon of Knowledge

AN IRISH FOLKTALE

retold by Matthew Richards • illustrated by Shane Clester

CHAPTER 1
THE LEGENDARY FINN MACCOOL

This is a tale of Finn MacCool, a famous Irish hero who lived in a far-off time. There are many tales that tell of Finn's daring and bravery, but let me tell you something of his early life and of how he gained wisdom. Some say the getting of wisdom was not of his own choosing, but who are we to decide what lies behind the choices a hero makes?

Before Finn was even born, his father Cumhaill was killed by the leader of a rival clan. Fearing that her life was in danger, his mother Muirrenn wrapped herself in a cloak and slipped away to the darkest part of the forest. There she hid until her child was born.

To keep her son safe from the rival clan, Muirren gave the boy to a foster family to raise. Because of his shining blond hair, he was nicknamed Finn (which means "fair one"), and the name stuck.

From an early age, Finn was tall and graceful, with great strength. He played with the animals in the forest, and soon he could outrun the deer, outjump the jackrabbbits, outclimb the squirrels, and outswim the fish. He had the skills to one day be the leader of his clan.

The one thing Finn did not have was wisdom. At that time, the wise men were the storytellers, and storytelling skills were just as important as physical skills. People were tested to see how many poems they could recite and how many tales they could tell.

One day, Finn gathered his forest friends around him.

"Let me tell you a story,
I'll try not to bore you,
Just please don't start snoring,
Until I am done.

I have not rehearsed this,
But I'll try for 12 verses,
I thought I had a story to tell,
But I find I have none... ouch!

Finn looked around and saw that the squirrels were throwing nuts at him. The rest of his audience was gone.

"Hmm," thought Finn to himself, "the rabbits taught me how to jump and the squirrels taught me how to climb. Who will teach me to be a singer of songs and a teller of tales? Who will give me the knowledge I lack?"

Finn asked his foster parents. His foster mother said, "We are simple folk. You must learn the storytelling arts from a wise man or woman."

"It is time for you to seek out Finnegas," said Finn's foster father. "He is a wise man and he can teach you to be a singer of songs and a teller of tales."

So Finn said good-bye to his foster parents and set off down the Boyne River to find the wise Finnegas.

CHAPTER 2
THE WISE FINNEGAS

Finnegas lived alone in a little house next to the Boyne River. As legend had it, the river led to a pool shaded by the Tree of Knowledge. The river was home to Fintan, the Salmon of Knowledge. It was said that the first person to eat the salmon would be given the gift of all knowledge. Finnegas had been trying to catch Fintan for seven long years.

Finn rowed his little round boat across the Boyne River to find Finnegas. He interrupted Finnegas just as he was pulling a dip net out of the water.

"Excuse me, Master Finnegas," said Finn. "People speak of you as a wise storyteller. I am eager to learn the storytelling arts. Would you agree to be my teacher?"

Finnegas agreed, and Finn began his studies. It soon became clear that Finn was not the best student. He had too much energy and would rather be hunting or playing games with other boys than studying.

One day, Finnegas surprised Finn in a clearing in the forest. He watched as Finn swung from tree branches, turned a few cartwheels, and chanted:

"I'm Finn MacCool and I'm no fool."

"I'm Finn MacCool and I've had enough of school."

"I'm Finn MacCool and I make my own rules."

Finnegas, exasperated, said, "Finn MacCool will obey *my* rules if he wants to go with me to the magic pool."

Finn immediately stopped his games. For weeks he had been begging Finnegas to let him go with him to the magic pool. Now, it seemed he would have his chance.

CHAPTER 3

CATCHING FINTAN

The next day, very early, Finnegas and Finn arrived at the magic pool near a bend in the Boyne River. Finnegas attached some bait to a basket trap and lowered it into the river.

"Now, we wait," said Finnegas.

"What do you think Fintan will taste like?" asked Finn. He loved food and was always curious about flavors.

"I have no interest in whether Fintan is flavorful," said Finnegas. "I am only concerned with all the things I will learn when I eat that fish."

Several hours went by. Finn spent the time sleeping, while Finnegas imagined what it would be like to be the wisest man in the world. Suddenly, his thoughts were interrupted by a splashing sound coming from the direction of the trap. The splashing grew louder, as though a large fish was thrashing inside the trap. Sure enough, when Finnegas and Finn hauled the trap up onto the riverbank, there was a great, silvery, spotted fish inside. It was Fintan.

"Well, Finn, it looks like you have been lucky for me. Would you like to cook this salmon? You are an excellent cook and I've never known you to burn anything.

"It would be an honor, Master Finnegas," said Finn.

"But you must be very careful. I particularly don't want any burned blisters on the skin. The salmon contains the knowledge I seek. If the skin blisters and pops, that knowledge may leak away. And Finn..."

"Yes, Master Finnegas?"

"Do not eat any part of this fish. Not the tiniest piece of flesh, not the smallest sliver of skin. Nothing. Do you understand?"

"Yes, Master Finnegas."

CHAPTER 4

THE BLISTER

Finn wanted to cook the fish perfectly for his teacher. He liked to do everything well. He put the salmon on a spit and turned it, being careful not to overcook it.

"What a luscious aroma," he said to himself. "I am sure that fish tastes better than anything I've ever eaten. If only I could have just one mouthful."

Just then, he noticed a blister beginning to form.

"What shall I do?" thought Finn in a panic. "Finnegas gave me clear instructions. No blisters. But there is a blister. And if it pops, some of the wisdom might leak out of Fintan. I wish I was wise enough to know what to do for the best."

Finn decided to press the blister very gently, just to let the air out. He touched the crispy hot skin with his thumb.

"Ouch!"

The hot juices from the salmon burned his thumb. Without thinking, he put his thumb into his mouth to cool it. As soon as his thumb was in his mouth, he wanted to know what the salmon tasted like. He sucked the juice from his thumb. Immediately, he felt as if he had been filled with a bright light. He knew immediately what had happened. In fact, he now knew *everything*!

One thing that Finn knew was that he couldn't undo what he had done. "Perhaps there is more wisdom to go around," he thought. But he knew that wasn't true.

Finn served Finnegas the salmon anyway. He presented it perfectly on a wooden platter.

Finnegas looked at the fish, then he looked at Finn.

"The skin seems to be unbroken," said Finnegas.

He turned the fish over to check the underside.

"No bites taken out of the flesh?"

"No, Master Finnegas."

Finally, Finnegas took a bite of the fish. He chewed. He swallowed. He waited. He wasn't sure what to expect.

After a long pause he said, "That's strange."

"What is strange?" asked Finn, innocently.

"I don't feel any different. I don't know much more than I did a minute ago. In fact, the only thing I know is that you look different. You have a strange light in your eye. Can it be...?"

Finn told Finnegas everything.

"In that case, there's nothing more I can teach you," said Finnegas. "You must go your own way, and may your new knowledge keep you safe."

Finn went on to have many adventures. He became a great leader of his people. And from that time on, whenever he sought knowledge, Finn had only to place his thumb in his mouth.

Summarize

Use details from *Finn MacCool and the Salmon of Knowledge* to summarize the story. Your chart may help you.

Details

↓

Point of View

Text Evidence

1. How can you tell that *Finn MacCool and the Salmon of Knowledge* is a folktale? Identify one feature that tells you this. GENRE

2. How does the narrator feel about Finn MacCool? Look at page 2 for clues. POINT OF VIEW

3. Find the word *knowledge* on page 4. How does knowing the root word help you figure out its meaning? ROOT WORDS

4. Write about how the story of Finn MacCool and the salmon would be different if Finnegas told the story. WRITE ABOUT READING

Compare Texts
Read about wild salmon and how to catch it.

Brain Food

Do you know why many people call salmon "brain food?" It's because many people think that eating salmon is good for your brain. In fact, many people think that wild salmon is one of the most healthful foods you can eat. It is full of a variety of fats that your brain needs to work well. One of these fats is called Omega 3. Wild salmon is also a very good source of protein. Throughout history, people have relied on fish for protein. Eating protein helps people to build their muscles and stay strong.

Salmon are found in the Pacific Ocean and the North Atlantic Ocean. Adult fish live in the ocean, but they swim to rivers to lay their eggs.

David Papazian/CORBIS

There are many ways to fish for salmon and other wild fish. Traditional methods include large traps or nets, fishing lines, spears, and baskets. Another method is to use a dip net to scoop the fish out of the water. If you want to try your hand at catching fish in a river or lake, here's how to make a dip net.

A dip net is a traditional way to catch wild salmon by scooping it out of the water.

Make a Dip Net

You Will Need

- 1 wire coat hanger
- needle and thread
- old hosiery
- string or tape
- a stick or rod

What to Do

1. Bend the coat hanger so that it is almost square.

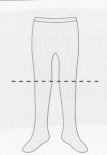

2. Cut the old hosiery halfway down the legs.

3. Tie the legs together. This will be the basket.

4. Place the old hosiery through the hanger and fold the waistband over the coat hanger.

5. Have an adult help you sew the hem around the coat hanger.

6. Attach the coat hanger to the stick using string or tape.

Make Connections

Why is wild salmon a good choice of fish to eat?
ESSENTIAL QUESTION

Why did the Irish choose salmon as the animal that gave knowledge? Use what you learned from *Finn MacCool and the Salmon of Knowledge* and *Brain Food* to support your response. **TEXT TO TEXT**

Focus on
Genre

Folktales Folktales are stories passed on from one person to the next by word of mouth or by oral tradition. Folktales are not realistic and can include talking animals, magical events, and larger-than-life characters.

Read and Find *Finn MacCool and the Salmon of Knowledge* is a folktale with a larger-than-life main character. He has super strength. He gains incredible wisdom.

Your Turn

Think of some of the qualities you possess. What would happen if those qualities were "larger than life?" Write a story in which you are the hero and you have one or more super powers.